C000149390

An Engineer's Journey in Mathland, Part 1

Province of the Balanced Ternary System

By: Hazem Mahsoub

FIRST EDITION

Dedication

To my father, the one who passed on
the passion for science and technology to me.

Acknowledgement

I'd like to express my deepest appreciation for my friends, Ahmed Saleh and Amr Yassin, who reviewed this book repeatedly, as well as Ali Elmeteiny for his great gift, the cover image and the 3D images.

Table of Content

Preface

Have you ever had an idea and became extremely excited about it, only to find out that it's not new and that others have had the same idea, or even did full implementation? This could be a big disappointment or a great validation of your thought process.

This is what happened to me.

I had an idea of a new numeral system and later of a new logic system, similar to the binary numeral system and Boolean logic and algebra. I got the idea from an ancient riddle and thought that it could be the basis of a computing system that's more efficient than the binary system. I've developed a mathematical proof, a validation of the system, then developed algorithms on how to do the basic math operations using this system and shared my work with a friend with a Ph.D. degree in math. He was impressed and I was super happy. A few days later, he told me he had found a similar system, identical to what I've called the M-System actually, called *the balanced ternary system* in an unpopular math reference.

I felt disappointed for a while then I decided to continue my work for two reasons:

1) The fun I had developing this system was better than any system I've developed. Yes, I am not a mathematician; my degree is in electronics engineering and all of my work experience has been in software engineering.

2) With my fresh pair of eyes, I had hopes that I'll develop something that hasn't been developed before and contribute to this hypothetical computing system. So, I've decided to solve the problem at hand and compare my work to the work of others but only at the end. Of course, that was a big risk, but I felt this was my best chance of new findings/design.

This work became my hobby, although I didn't give it as much time as I wanted to until recently. Earning a living in a field where there are always new technologies to learn has been a challenge.

Every now and then, I'd go back to what I've written and find some parts that felt like lame ideas and some parts that I find too good not to be completed. So, whenever I had a chance to continue my work, I did. That was done over a long period of time which also meant the fresh pair of eyes were always fresh and sometimes I couldn't pick up where I left, and a new direction appeared.

The realization at the end that some parts are totally novel was a great satisfaction.

'Hope you enjoy the book and find it inspiring.

About This Book Series

The Name of The Book Series

My smart nephew asked me once about what I was working on and I said "This could be a great invention. Wish me luck!". "An invention or a discovery?", he asked.

I don't remember my immediate reply to him, but I kept thinking about his question afterwards. I consider math a natural thing that has been and will be always there. So, if I come up with a new way to do some calculation should that be a discovery or an invention? The implementation, though, may be more of an invention than a discovery.

When the first parts came to an end, I remembered our discussion and decided to give it the name:

"An Engineer's Journey in Mathland"

As you will see, my approach has been more of an engineer than a mathematician and it has been an exploration journey more than anything else.

As for the question "Is it an invention or a discovery?", I'd better leave it to the reader to answer.

What Is This Book Series About

Here is the main idea:

The vast majority of today's computers are based on three pillars:

- The binary numeral system.
- Boolean logic and algebra.
- The transistor circuits.

The perfect match among these three systems -0/1 matches true/false, matches on/off- is *the key* to the great success of today's computers.

So, for a computer based on the balanced ternary system to succeed, we must develop logic and algebra to match it, as well as a matching implementation.

Part one focuses on the balanced ternary system, part two focuses on 3-value logic, and part three focuses on the implementation.

Prerequisites

As you may have guessed, this book assumes the reader is already familiar with:

1) For part 1: numeral systems, such as decimal, binary, and ternary systems. Octal and hexadecimal systems are also good to be familiar with. The main idea is the familiarity with doing basic math in systems other than decimal, as well as conversion among them.

2) For part 2: Boolean logic and algebra.

There are hundreds of books on these topics, as well as online resources. It would have been redundant to try to cover them here. It's recommended to refresh your knowledge in these topics before starting on this book.

How Is This Book Series Organized

The first few drafts of this book were written as a textbook explaining the newly developed system. When I found out that a big chunk of the work[1] has been developed before, I thought of taking all these parts out. That would have left out a lot of context and made the book unreadable to the majority.

Then, I thought of narrating the story of this research as it has developed, highlighting the sections that are believed to be novel and couldn't be found in any reference. This way, the reader can better follow the flow of thoughts and connect how all of these pieces fit together. That is, the default for all sections is that they have been developed before unless otherwise is stated.

Another reason for taking this route is that the prerequisite knowledge of the binary and ternary numeral system, as well as Boolean algebra. So, excluding the prerequisites and including the parts that were developed by others is kind of a halfway solution.

The Series Parts

The book series has three parts:

- The balanced ternary system
- 3-value logic and algebra
- Implementation

In the first part, we will start by the ancient riddle and how it led to developing the new numeral system. At the beginning, I called it the *M-System* then I found out that great mathematicians have developed it long before me. Although most of it has been developed before, it had to be covered in the book since it is the basis for an important discussion down the road.

The second part discusses logic and algebra where there are 3 possible values. At the beginning, I called it *Mahsoubean logic and algebra* then found out about the work of others in that space. The starting point for me -and for others before me- has been borrowing definitions and functions from Boolean logic. This led to a roadblock that needed a big shift.

[1] https://en.wikipedia.org/wiki/Balanced_ternary

This shift paved the way to put down new equations that will make the implementation of our hypothetical system possible. This part is the core of the whole research.

The third part discusses the implementation of the basic "circuits" and how they're used to build circuits that can perform math operations. It also discusses if transistor circuits are the best match and other possibilities.

Sequence

It's highly recommended to read the book chapters in sequence. One of the objectives of adopting the journey theme is that the reader will gain familiarity and build up his/her knowledge as he/she moves from one chapter to the next.

If the reader is familiar with the balanced ternary system, he/she can quickly read through the first part or skip it altogether. I'll try to highlight some sections and provide cross-references to give the reader the freedom to skip chapters although reading in sequence is highly recommended.

Examples

In many cases, the most efficient way to explain a point was through examples, especially the first part. Feel free to skip these examples/exercises if you've already got the point.

Your Feedback

Your feedback is highly appreciated.

As I have disclaimed earlier, I've discovered that some parts and algorithms were developed by others before me, while other parts I believe I am the first to develop.

Your feedback is highly appreciated on validating what's novel, what's not, in addition to any errors, as well as improvement suggestions.

'Hope you enjoy the book and find it inspiring. We've only scratched the surface. There's a lot of work to be done for our hypothetical computer system to catch up and become as mature as today's binary computers.

Chapter 1.01:
The Start - An Old Riddle

The Start - An Old Riddle

The exploration journey started with a riddle. During California's rolling blackouts in the late 90s, and more importantly Internet outages, solving riddles was the best thing a group of developers could come up with.

Here is the riddle:

> *A fruit merchant used a balance scale to weigh the fruits he's selling. He wanted to have the smallest number of iron weights to carry with him. His question was: "What is the smallest number of weights I need, to be able to weigh fruits from 1 kilogram to 40 kilograms?"*

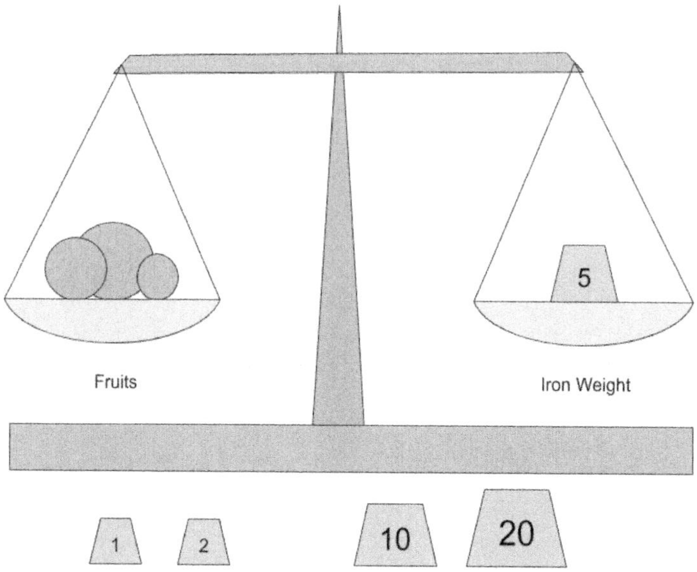

Figure 1.01.01: Balance Scale with Fruits and Iron Weights

Thinking of money bills, someone started by suggesting the following: 1 kg, 2 * 2 kg, 5 kg, 10 kg, and 20 kg. That's 6 weights.

Someone else was thinking of the binary system and suggested 1 kg, 2 kg, 4 kg, 8 kg, 16 kg, 32 kg. That's also 6 weights but covers from 1 kg to 63 kg.

The best answer was 4 weights, *only 4 weights*: 1 kg, 3 kg, 9 kg, and 27 kg.

The trick here is that the merchant can put the iron weights on both sides: the empty side, as well as the side of the fruits.

For Example, if the bag of fruits weighs 2 kg, the used weights are 1 kg on the side of the fruits and 3 kg on the other side.

If the bag of fruits weighs 5 kg, the used weights are 1 kg, 3 kg on the side of the fruits and 9 kg on the other side.

Range of weights covered:

Using 1 kg and 3 kg the merchant can cover 1 kg, 2 kg, 3 kg, and 4 kg.

If we add 9 kg to that, we cover from 1 kg to 13 kg which is the total sum of all weights, and so on. The next weight that can be added should be double the sum of all lesser weights plus one. That is 2*13+1 = 27.

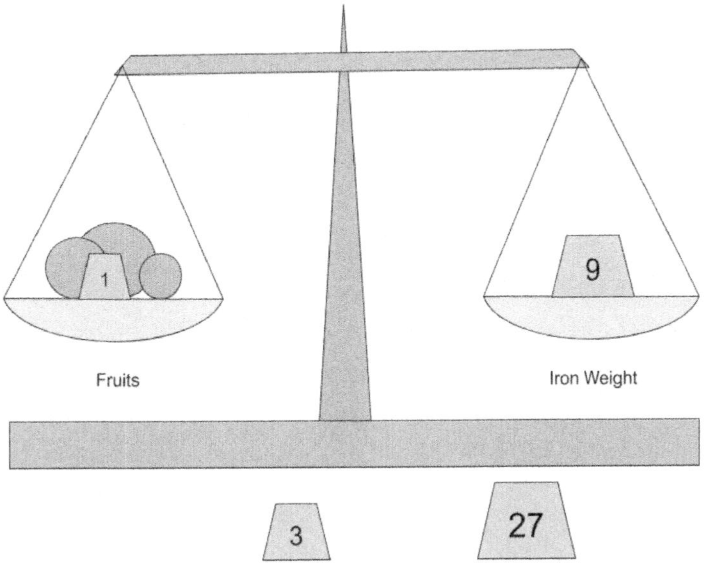

Figure 1.01.02: Best Solution for Iron Weights

A New Numeral System

The fact that the weights formed a geometric series, of basis 3, intrigued me and made me think of the ternary system.

Here, the basis, 3, comes from the *three* places where an iron weight can be:

- on the fruit's side,
- on the opposite side,
- or on neither.

That corresponds to values -1, 1, or 0, respectively.

What if we build a numeral system similar to the ternary system with the following conditions:

1) Each digit is 3 times the value of the digit to its right, similar to the ternary system;

2) Each digit can have a value of 0, 1, or -1, that's different from the ternary system.

I tried to represent a few numbers using this system, with the balance scale in mind, and it worked out fine.

That's good but I needed to prove that it will always work. So, I developed the proof you find in the following chapters.

Then, I went a step further and generalized the new system where a single digit can be positive, zero, or negative, and came to good governing rules. You can read more about it in the following chapters.

The proof in the following chapter, as well as the generalization or expansion of the balanced ternary system are novel, I believe. Basic math using the new numeral system must have been developed by others long before me[2]. What I couldn't find anywhere and believe is novel and more efficient are the steps, or algorithm, on how to do long division and conversion from decimal.

Side Note:

This numeral system may remind us of the Roman numeral system since some written numbers must be subtracted to get the value of the whole number. However, this numeral system is way more efficient when used in basic math operations.

Now, let's get familiar with the new system.

[2] https://en.wikipedia.org/wiki/Balanced_ternary

Chapter 1.02: Getting Familiar with the Balanced Ternary System

Getting Familiar with the Balanced Ternary System

I've used the letter M to represent -1, i.e. short for **M**inus one, since it's only one character and will fit perfectly into one digit. In fact, I was naming this system *the M-System*. Later, I found out that others have used an inverted '1' to represent -1 as well as '-' and '+' to represent -1 and +1.

'M' is still the easiest method that can be used on all word processors and will be used in this book.

As you will see, the following features and basic characteristics in this chapter are direct inference/deduction from the basic definition of the balanced ternary system, or in short BT system.

As we mentioned earlier, there are two constraints in this system:

1) Each digit is 3 times the value of the digit to its right.

2) Each digit can have a value of 0, 1, or -1.

So, if we have one digit, we can represent 3 numbers: -1, 0, and 1.

If we have two digits, we can represent 9 numbers: from -4 to +4 as follows:

BT system[3]	Conversion	Decimal system
MM_M	-3-1	-4
$M0_M$	-3+0	-3
$M1_M$	-3+1	-2
$0M_M$	0-1	-1
00_M	0+0	0
01_M	0+1	1
$1M_M$	3-1	2
10_M	3+0	3
11_M	3+1	4

[3] BT system stands for balanced ternary system.

The Rotating Odometer

When we look at the list of numbers in the first column, we can visualize an odometer where each digit has the values M, 0, and 1. When the odometer rotates the M comes after the 1. At this point the digit to the left will be changing too.

So, in addition to the balance scale, we have this rotating odometer to think of as a physical representation of our system.

Figure 1.02.01: Hypothetical Rotating Odometer

We notice that for n digits, the numbers that can be represented are 3^n, which is always an odd number: the number of positive numbers equals the number of negative numbers plus the number zero.

The range of numbers that can be represented starts from $-(3^n-1)/2$ to $+(3^n-1)/2$.

Basic Conversion

To make sure we have a good grasp of the balanced ternary system, let's examine the conversion of 3-digit numbers from the BT system to the decimal system. We start by the smallest number, i.e. MMM.

$MMM_M = (-1) * 3^2 + (-1) * 3^1 + (-1) * 3^0 = -9 -3 -1 = -13$
$MM0_M = (-1) * 3^2 + (-1) * 3^1 + (\ 0) * 3^0 = -9 -3 +0 = -12$
$MM1_M = (-1) * 3^2 + (-1) * 3^1 + (+1) * 3^0 = -9 -3 +1 = -11$

$M0M_M = (-1) * 3^2 + (0) * 3^1 + (-1) * 3^0 = -9 +0 -1 = -10$
$M00_M = (-1) * 3^2 + (0) * 3^1 + (\ 0) * 3^0 = -9 +0 +0 = -9$

$M01_M = (-1) * 3^2 + (0) * 3^1 + (+1) * 3^0 = -9 +0 +1 = -8$

$M1M_M = (-1) * 3^2 + (+1) * 3^1 + (-1) * 3^0 = -9 +3 -1 = -7$
$M10_M = (-1) * 3^2 + (+1) * 3^1 + (0) * 3^0 = -9 +3 +0 = -6$
$M11_M = (-1) * 3^2 + (+1) * 3^1 + (+1) * 3^0 = -9 +3 +1 = -5$

$0MM_M = (0) * 3^2 + (-1) * 3^1 + (-1) * 3^0 = 0 -3 -1 = -4$
$0M0_M = (0) * 3^2 + (-1) * 3^1 + (0) * 3^0 = 0 -3 +0 = -3$
$0M1_M = (0) * 3^2 + (-1) * 3^1 + (+1) * 3^0 = 0 -3 +1 = -2$

$00M_M = (0) * 3^2 + (0) * 3^1 + (-1) * 3^0 = 0 +0 -1 = -1$
$000_M = (0) * 3^2 + (0) * 3^1 + (0) * 3^0 = 0 +0 +0 = 0$
$001_M = (0) * 3^2 + (0) * 3^1 + (+1) * 3^0 = 0 +0 +1 = 1$

$01M_M = (0) * 3^2 + (+1) * 3^1 + (-1) * 3^0 = 0 +3 -1 = 2$
$010_M = (0) * 3^2 + (+1) * 3^1 + (0) * 3^0 = 0 +3 +0 = 3$
$011_M = (0) * 3^2 + (+1) * 3^1 + (+1) * 3^0 = 0 +3 +1 = 4$

$1MM_M = (+1) * 3^2 + (-1) * 3^1 + (-1) * 3^0 = 9 -3 -1 = 5$
$1M0_M = (+1) * 3^2 + (-1) * 3^1 + (0) * 3^0 = 9 -3 +0 = 6$
$1M1_M = (+1) * 3^2 + (-1) * 3^1 + (+1) * 3^0 = 9 -3 +1 = 7$

$10M_M = (+1) * 3^2 + (0) * 3^1 + (-1) * 3^0 = 9 +0 -1 = 8$
$100_M = (+1) * 3^2 + (0) * 3^1 + (0) * 3^0 = 9 +0 +0 = 9$
$101_M = (+1) * 3^2 + (0) * 3^1 + (+1) * 3^0 = 9 +0 +1 = 10$

$11M_M = (+1) * 3^2 + (+1) * 3^1 + (-1) * 3^0 = 9 +3 -1 = 11$
$110_M = (+1) * 3^2 + (+1) * 3^1 + (0) * 3^0 = 9 +3 +0 = 12$
$111_M = (+1) * 3^2 + (+1) * 3^1 + (+1) * 3^0 = 9 +3 +1 = 13$

Nice Feature of the Geometric Series

One of the features of our 3-based geometric series is that the sum of its terms is smaller than half of the next term.

In our balance scale as a physical illustration of the BT system, if we have 4 pieces of iron weights:1, 3, 9, 27 the sum of which is 40. That's less than half of the next weight which is 81. To generalize the rule for any number of weights:

Sum of n weights = $1*3^0 + 1*3^1 + 1*3^2 + ...+ 1*3^{(n-1)}$

$$= \sum_{i=1}^{n} 3^{i-1} = (3^n-1)/(3-1) = (3^n-1)/2$$

That's definitely less than the next term, which is 3^n. In other words, any weight will be larger than double the sum of all smaller weights by 1.

This will come in handy in basic math operations.

Reading the Sign of a Number

Since the digits themselves can be positive or negative, the sign is embedded in the number. Here are the rules to follow:

1) If the most significant digit is 1, it's a positive number.
2) If the most significant digit is M, it's a negative number.
3) If it's zero it's zero. Note how significant it is to represent zero as a non-positive non-negative number.

Thinking of the balance scale, we've already established that any weight is larger than double the sum of all smaller weights by one. Hence, we can safely say that the sign of the most significant digit is the sign of the whole number, irrespective of the less significant digits.

Example:

What is the sign of the following numbers: 1M100, M11, 0000?

Solution:

```
1M100 is positive.

M11 is negative.

0000 is zero.
```

[To verify, convert to decimal.]

Changing the Sign of a Number

To change the sign of a number turn each 1 into M, each M into 1, and leave zeros as is. This feature will come in handy implementing subtraction.[4]

[4] Thinking of binary and the two's complement, I've always found it brilliant but ugly. Changing the sign in the

Thinking of the balance scale, this is equivalent to switching all iron weights from each side to the opposite side.

Example:

Change the sign of the numbers: M101, 110M.

Solution:

```
M101 => 1M0M

110M => MM01
```

[To verify, convert to decimal.]

Comparing Two Numbers

Rules:

1) M < 0 < 1
2) If both numbers have the same number of digits, i.e. same length, start by comparing the most significant digit then comparing the next digit until you reach a result.
3) If two numbers have different number of digits, then:
    a) If the most significant digit of the longer number is M, it is the smaller number.
    b) If the most significant digit of the longer number is 1, it is the larger number.

Example:

Compare the numbers: 1M with 10, 1MM with 11, and M1M with MM.

Solution:

```
1M < 10

1MM > 11

M1M < MM
```

[To verify, convert to decimal.]

Largest/Smallest Number of N Digits

- The largest number of n digits has 1 in all digits.
- The smallest number of n digits has M in all digits, not zero.
- The largest *negative* number of n digits starts by M followed by 1s in the remaining digits.
- The smallest *positive* number of n digits starts by 1 followed by Ms in the remaining digits.

Example:

What are the largest positive and negative numbers of 5 digits?

What are the smallest positive and negative numbers of 4 digits?

Solution:

Largest positive number of 5 digits is 11111_M.

Largest negative number of 5 digits is $M1111_M$.

Smallest positive number of 4 digits is $1MMM_M$.

Smallest negative number of 4 digits is $MMMM_M$.

[To verify, look at the next, or previous, number and verify they have different number of digits.]

Direction and Magnitude

When we say 'larger' or 'smaller' we typically mean direction, i.e. more towards positive infinity or negative infinity. In the following chapters we will make a distinction between direction and magnitude.

To compare the magnitude of two numbers of different signs, it would be easier to change the sign of one of them then apply the comparison rules.

Example:

Which number is larger in magnitude: 1MM or M10?

Solution:

1) Change the sign of the second number: `M10 => 1M0`.

2) Compare both numbers: `1MM < 1M0`.

   `That is, 1MM is larger in magnitude than M10.`

   [To verify, convert to decimal.]

Chapter 1.03:
Basic Mathematical Operations

Basic Mathematical Operations

To make sure that our system is valid and practical to use, the next step had to be developing rules, steps, and algorithms to perform basic operations. As expected, the division was the most challenging one. The steps, or the algorithm, for division couldn't be found anywhere and believe it's novel.

Addition

Rules:

1) The sum of any digit and zero is the digit.
2) The sum of 1 and M is zero.
3) The sum of 1 and 1 is M *with carry of 1.*
4) The sum of M and M is 1 *with carry of M.*

Example:

What is the sum of M10 and M11?

Solution:

```
1    <-- Carry
M10
M11  [add]
----
MM1
```

[To verify, convert all numbers to decimal]

Subtraction

Steps:

1) Change the sign of the number to be subtracted, as explained in the previous chapter.
2) Add it to the first number.

Example:

Subtract 1MM from M10.

Solution:

1) Change the sign of the number to be subtracted.

```
1MM => M11
```

2) Add it to the first number.

```
1     <-- Carry
M10
1MM  [subtract]
M11  [add]
----
MM1
```

[To verify, convert all numbers to decimal]

Multiplication

Rules:

1) The product of any digit and zero is zero.
2) The product of any digit and 1 is the digit.
3) The product of M and M is 1.

Notice that the product of any two digits is also one digit, i.e. no carry.

Example:

Multiply M101 by 10M

Solution:

```
  M101
   10M    [multiply]
 ------
  1M0M
 00000    [add]
M10100    [add]
 ------
M1100M
```

[To verify, convert to decimal.]

Divisibility

Rules:

1) A number is divisible by 3 if the least significant digit is zero.
2) A number is divisible by 3^n if the least significant n digits are zeros.
3) A number is divisible by 2, i.e. even number, if the sum of the number of 1s plus the sum of the number of Ms is an even number. Otherwise, it's an odd number.
   That is, count the number of 1s in the number and count the number of Ms. If the total of both is even then the number is even. If the total of both is odd, then the number is odd.

Example:

Which of the following numbers is odd and which is even: M101, 1MMM, 10?

Solution:

M101 => one M + two 1s = 3 => **odd**
1MMM => one 1 + three Ms =4 => **even**
10 => one 1 =1 => **odd**
[To verify, convert to decimal.]

Division

Steps:

1) Starting from the LHS, take a segment of the dividend, with the same length as the divisor, and compare it to the divisor:
   a) If the segment is smaller *magnitude-wise* put 0 as the division result and bring down the next digit to the right of the segment.
   b) If the segment and the divisor have the same sign, the result is 1.
   c) If the signs differ, the result is M.
2) Now, multiply the result by the divisor and subtract it from the segment.
3) *If the remainder is still equal to or larger than the divisor, repeat the previous step , i.e. divide the remainder, and write the result of the division as a carry above the previous resulting digit. Multiply the result by the divisor and subtract it again until the result is magnitude-wise smaller than the divisor.*
4) Bring down the next digit to the right of the remainder.
5) Divide the new segment by the divisor.

6) Repeat the previous steps until the remainder is zero and there are no digits left in the dividend to process, whichever is later.
7) In case you have a remainder after reaching the end of the dividend, you may continue by adding a fraction point and zeros.

One point to highlight here is that the objective of the division of the segment is to drive the remainder closer to zero. That is, we care here about the *magnitude*, not the *direction*.

Second point to highlight here is that the carry is put above the same digit in the result, not above the digit to the left of it, as we do in addition!!

Last point: In long division, the main steps are *divide*, *multiply*, *subtract*, and *bring down* the next digit. The only difference here is that the division result can be one or two digits. Hence, the division may be repeated resulting in a carry. This is much simpler than the method used today of comparing the dividend to the divisor and to half of the divisor.

> **Side Note**:
>
> When long division is taught to little children the phrase they memorize is *daddy-mommy-sister-brother*, since they have the same first letter of the main steps. Consider the added step, the carry, is *the cousin* in the memorable phrase.

Example #1:

Divide 10M by 1M.

Solution:

```
            11
         ________
1M      | 10M
 _______| 1M  —[write the product here to be subtracted]
          M1   [subtract, i.e. change the sign then add]
         ___
          01M
           1M —[write the product here to be subtracted]
           M1  [subtract, i.e. change the sign then add]
          ___
           00
```

The result is **11**.
[To verify, convert to decimal.]

Example #2:

Divide 10M by 11.

Solution:

```
        1M
     ┌────
  11 │ 10M
  ───┘ 11 ──[write the product here to be subtracted]
       MM   [subtract, i.e. change the sign then add]
      ───
       0MM
        MM──[write the product here to be subtracted]
        11  [subtract, i.e. change the sign then add]
        ──
        00
```

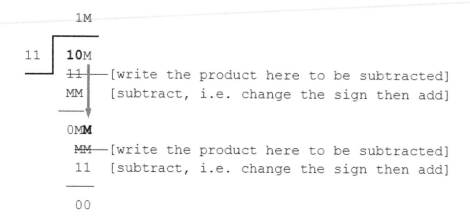

The result is **1M**.
[To verify, convert to decimal.]

Example #3:

Divide 101 by 1M.

Solution:

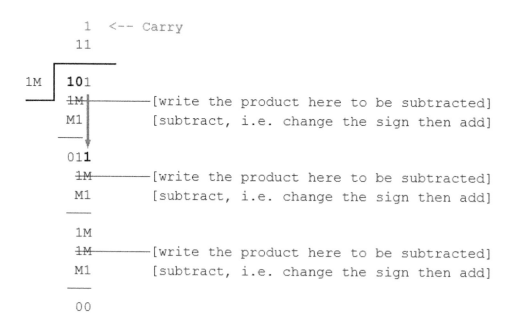

```
          1  <-- Carry
         11
     ┌──────
  1M │  101
  ───┘  1M ──────[write the product here to be subtracted]
        M1       [subtract, i.e. change the sign then add]
       ───
        011
         1M──────[write the product here to be subtracted]
         M1      [subtract, i.e. change the sign then add]
         ──
         1M
         1M──────[write the product here to be subtracted]
         M1      [subtract, i.e. change the sign then add]
         ──
         00
```

The result is 1 plus 11 = **1MM**.
[To verify, convert to decimal.]

Example #4:

Divide 10010 by 1M.

Solution:

```
              1       <-- Carry
            1110
         ________
   1M   | 10010
          1M      [write the product here to be subtracted]
          M1      [subtract, i.e. change the sign then add]
          ——
          010
           1M     [write the product here to be subtracted]
           M1     [subtract, i.e. change the sign then add]
           ——
           011
            1M    [write the product here to be subtracted]
            M1    [subtract, i.e. change the sign then add]
            ——
            1M    [still equal or larger than the divisor]
            1M    [write the product here to be subtracted]
            M1    [subtract, i.e. change the sign then add]
            ——
            000
             00
             ——
             00
```

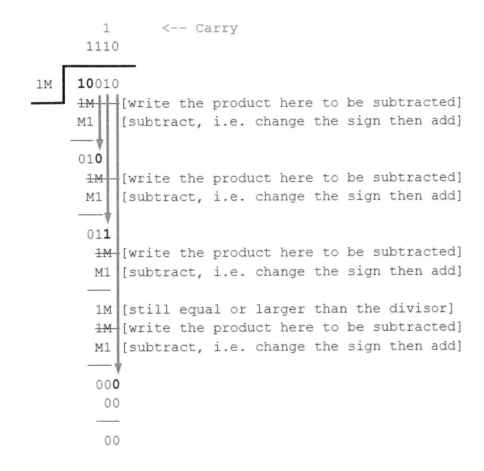

The result is 1110 plus 10.

```
  11     <-- Carry
  1110
    10   [add]
 ______
 1MMM0
```

The result is **1MMM0**.
[To verify, convert to decimal.]

Fractions

Since the base of this system is 3, then 0.1_M simply means one third and $0.M_M$ means negative one third.

The same conversion rules still apply beyond the fraction point.

Example:

Convert the following fraction to decimal: $0.1MM1_M$

Solution:

$0.1MM1_M = 1*3^{-1} -1*3^{-2} -1*3^{-3} +1*3^{-4} = 1/3 -1/9 -1/27 +1/81$

=

$=(27-9-3+1)/81 =$ **16/81**

Side Note:

Funny thing about fractions here is that the simplest fraction in decimal is not so simple in the BT system. By that I mean 1/2, or half. It's equal to 0.1111111111 and as the number of 1s increases the closer we get to one half exactly!

Actually, it is somewhere between 0.1111111111 and 1.MMMMMMMMMM.

Chapter 1.04: Conversions

Conversions

The following diagram illustrates the conversion paths among various numeral systems. As the diagram shows, conversions from/to binary and BT systems are not straightforward but it can be done by doing conversion to the decimal system first. Conversions between decimal and ternary or binary are already covered by several books and online resources such that we can safely skip. We will only focus on conversion from/to the BT system.

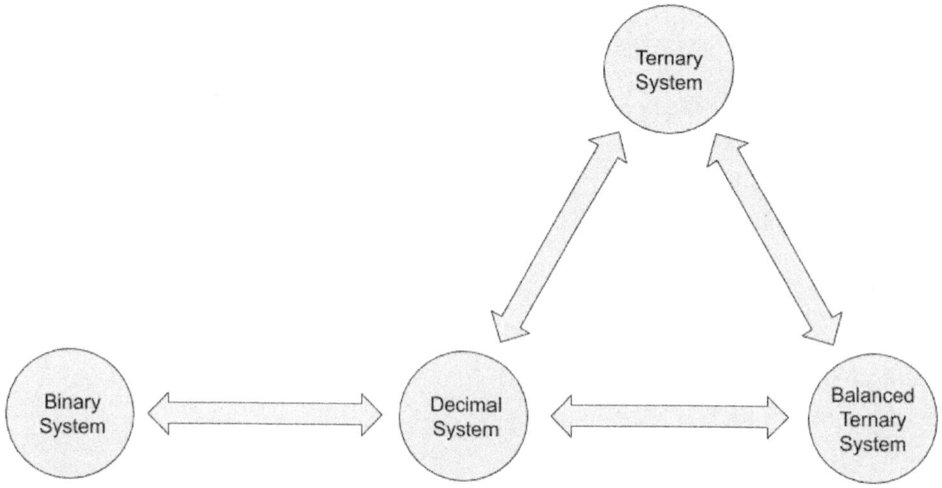

Figure 1.04.01: Conversions Among Numeral Systems

From BT System to Ternary System

Steps:

1) Separate the negative digits from the positive digits.
2) Convert both to ternary.
3) Subtract the negative number from the positive number.

Example:

Convert $1M101_M$ to the ternary system.

Solution:

1) $1M101_M = 10101_M + 0M000_M$
2) $= 10101_3 - 01000_3$

```
10101
01000        [subtract]
------
02101
```

The result is **2101_3**.

[To verify, convert to decimal]

From Ternary System to BT System

Steps:

1) Every 2 should be converted to an M with a carry of 1. 1s and 0s stay the same.
2) Add the carries to the new number.

Example:

Convert 10212_3 to the BT system.

Solution:

1) 10212_3 => `10M1M with carry of 1 above 1 and 0`

2)
```
  1 1       <-- carry
 10M1M      [add]
 ______
 11MMM
```

The result is **$11MMM_M$**.

[To verify, convert to decimal]

From BT System to Decimal

Steps (same as from ternary system):

1) Multiply each value of the digits by 3 to the power of the digit's position, starting by zero.
2) Add all digits.

Example:

Convert M10MM to decimal.

Solution:

$M10M_M = (-1)*3^0 + (0)*3^1 + (1)*3^2 + (-1)*3^3 = -1 + 0 + 9 - 27 = -19$

From Decimal to BT System[5]

Steps:

1) Imagine a ruler with marks at 3^n. For example:1, 3, 9, 27, 81. The decimal number may match a mark or lie between two of them.
2) If it matches a mark, we have completed our conversion.
3) If not, determine if it's closer to the upper mark or the lower mark. In other words, compare it to the midpoint between the marks. That will determine which mark will be used. Notice that we always have odd numbers, i.e. midpoint is always some integer and a half.
4) Calculate the difference and repeat the same steps on the difference.
5) Form a series of numbers, of the used marks, that added/subtracted together will give us our decimal number.
6) Write in the form of sum of multiples of 3 and convert it to BT system.

Example:

Convert 22 from the decimal system to BT system.

Solution:

1) Compare it to 1,3,9,27,81. It lies between 9 and 27. Compare it to 13.5, which is half of 27. It's greater than 13.5, so we will use 27. The difference is 5 (=27-22).
   $22 = 27 - 5$
2) Compare 5 to our marks; it lies between 3 and 9 and is greater than 4.5. So we will use 9 and the difference is 4 (=9-5).
   $22 = 27 - (9-4)$
3) Compare 4 to our marks; it lies between 3 and 9 and less than 4.5. So, we will use 3 and the difference is 1 (=4-3).
   $22 = 27 - (9 - (3+1))$
4) Compare 1 to our marks, it is exactly 1. Stop repeating the steps and convert to BT system.
   $22 = 27 -9 +3 +1$
   $= 1*3^3 -1*3^2+1*3^1+1*3^0$
   $= 1M11_M$

   The result is **$1M11_M$**.
   [To verify, convert back to decimal]

Alternative approach:

There is always the other route of converting from decimal to ternary and then to balanced ternary system, as shown in the diagram at the beginning.

---

[5] Couldn't find these conversion steps, or algorithm, anywhere and believe it's novel.

Chapter 1.05:
Validating the Balanced Ternary System

Validating the Balanced Ternary System[6]

To prove the validity of the BT system, it's enough to prove one-to-one mapping with a valid system, such as the decimal system. One-to-one mapping can be defined as:

1) There are no gaps, i.e. all numbers are mapped.
2) There is only one number in the BT system that corresponds to each number in a valid system, such as the decimal system.

Proof:

1) For one digit, the numbers are M, 0, and 1.

   The difference between M and 0 is 1 and the difference between 0 and 1 is 1.

   That is, for one digit, all numbers between -1 and 1 are mapped to the BT system. No integers are skipped and there is one-to-one mapping.

2) For n digits:

   $\because M < 0 < 1$

   $\therefore$ the largest number in the BT system that can be represented by n digits has 1 in all digits ($111..1_M$) and the smallest number is ($MM...M_M$).

3) That is, the smallest positive number in the BT system that can be represented by n digits is '1' followed by Ms in the remaining digits ($1MM..M_M$) and the largest negative number in the BT system by n digits is M followed by 1s ($M11..1_M$).

Note that, in other all-positive systems, the smallest number is always zero.

Read the following row by row:

For n digits, the largest (most positive) number is $11...1_M$= $= 1*3^0 + 1*3^1 + 1*3^2 + ...+ 1*3^{(n-1)}$ $= \sum_{i=0}^{n-1} 3^i = (3^n-1)/(3-1)$ $= (3^n-1)/2$ We will call this number K	For n digits, the smallest (most negative) number is $MM...M_M$= $= (-1)*3^0 + (-1)*3^1 + (-1)*3^2 + ...+(-1)*3^{(n-1)}$ $= \sum_{i=0}^{n-1}(-1)*3^i = (-1)*(3^n-1)/(3-1)$ $= (-1)(3^n-1)/2 = (1-3^n)/2$ We will call this number V
For n+1 digits, the smallest positive number is $1MM...M_M$= $= 1*3^n +$ (the smallest number of n digits)	For n+1 digits, the largest negative number is $M11...1_M$= $= (-1)*3^n +$(the largest number of n digits)

[6] Couldn't find this proof anywhere and believe it's novel.

$= 1*3^n + (1-3^n)/2$ $= 3^n + (1-3^n)/2$ We will call this number L	$= (-1)*3^n + (3^n-1)/2$ $= -3^n + (3^n-1)/2$ We will call this number W
The difference between L and K = $= 1MM..M_M - 11..1_M$ $= 3^n + (1-3^n)/2 - (3^n-1)/2$ $= 3^n + (1-3^n)/2 + (1-3^n)/2$ $= 3^n + (1-3^n) =$ **1** That is, no numbers are skipped or have dual representation in the BT system.	The difference between W and V = $= M11..1_M - MM..M_M$ $= (-3^n + (3^n-1)/2) - (1-3^n)/2$ $= (-3^n + (3^n-1)/2) + (3^n-1)/2$ $= -3^n + (3^n-1) =$ **-1** That is, no numbers are skipped or have dual representation in the BT system.

∵ the difference is constant and is equal to one, or minus one.

∴ there is exactly one representation in the BT system for each decimal number.

That is, all numbers are covered.

Chapter 1.06: Generalization of Positive/Negative Numeral Systems

Generalization of Positive/Negative Numeral Systems[7]

At this stage of my journey, I took a wrong turn in an attempt to generalize the BT system. However, after correcting that wrong turn, we ended up with good governing rules for generalizing what I called *the positive/negative numeral systems*.

A Wrong Turn

First attempt at Generalization

In that attempt, I've changed one of the conditions of the BT system:

Each digit can be -2, -1, 0, 1, 2.

Let's use N to represent -2, in addition to M for -1, and call this system *the N-System.*

Originally, I was naming the BT system the M-System before I knew its common name.

Now, let's apply our previous proof to validate the N-System:

1) For one digit, the numbers that can be represented are N, M, 0, 1, and 2.

   The difference between each successive 2 numbers is 1.

   ∴ For the range covered by 1 digit, i.e. -2 till 2, all numbers are mapped, no skipping and no double mapping.

2) For n digits:

   ∵ N < M < 0 < 1 < 2

   ∴ the largest number that can be represented by n digits is $22..2_N$ and the smallest $NN..N_N$.

For n digits, the largest (most positive) number is $22...2_N$= $= 2*3^0 + 2*3^1 + 2*3^2 + ...+ 2*3^{(n-1)}$ $= 2*\sum_{i=0}^{n-1} 3^i = 2*(3^n-1)/(3-1) = (3^n-1)$ We will call this number K	For n digits, the smallest (most negative) number is $NN...N_N$= $= (-2)*3^0 + (-2)*3^1 + (-2)*3^2 + ...+ (-2)*3^{(n-1)}$ $= \sum_{i=0}^{n-1}(-2)*3^i = (-2)*(3^n-1)/(3-1) = (-2)(3^n-1)/2$ $= (1-3^n)$ We will call this number V
For n+1 digits, the smallest positive number is $1NN...N_N$ $= 1*3^n$ +(the smallest number of n digits)	For n+1 digits, the largest negative number is $M22...2_N$= $= (-1)*3^n$ +(the largest number of n digits)

[7] Couldn't find these steps for generalization anywhere and believe it's novel.

$= 1*3^n + (1-3^n)$ $= 3^n + (1-3^n) = 1$ We will call this number L	$= (-1)*3^n + (3^n-1)$ $= -3^n + (3^n-1) = -1$ We will call this number W
The difference between L and K = $= 1NN..N_N - 22..2_N$ $= 1 - (3^n-1)$ $= 1 - 3^n + 1$ $= 2 - 3^n$ That is, the difference is not constant and can be negative, i.e. there could be two representations of some numbers: one of n digits and one of n+1 digits.	The difference between W and V = $=N22..2_N - NN..N_N$ $= -1 -(1-3^n)$ $= -2 + 3^n$ $= 3^n - 2$ That is, the difference is not constant and can be positive, i.e. there could be two representations of some numbers: one of n digits and one of n+1 digits.

So, that system has failed our test!!

As an example of a failed one-to-one mapping: 1 can be represented by 1_N or $1N_N$.

Correcting the Wrong Turn

Maybe we should change the other condition as well.

That is, maybe if we increase the base of the system the overlap will disappear. Since the range covered by one digit is 5 maybe the basis should be 5. Instead of trial and error, let's use our proof to guide us toward the correct base:

For n digits, the largest (most positive) number is $22...2_N$= $= 2*B^0 + 2*B^1 + 2*B^2 + ...+ 2*B^{(n-1)}$ $= 2*\sum_{i=0}^{n-1} B^i = 2*(B^n-1)/(B-1)$ We will call this number K	For n digits, the smallest (most negative) number is $NN...N_N$= $= (-2)*B^0 + (-2)*B^1 + (-2)*B^2 + ...+ (-2)*B^{(n-1)}$ $= \sum_{i=0}^{n-1} (-2)*B^i = (-2)*(B^n-1)/(B-1)$ We will call this number V
For n+1 digits, the smallest positive number is $1NN...N_N$ $= 1*B^n$ + (the smallest number of n digits) $= 1*B^n - 2*(B^n-1)/(B-1)$ $= B^n - 2*(B^n-1)/(B-1)$ We will call this number L	For n+1 digits, the largest negative number is $M22...2_N$= $= (-1)*B^n$ +(the largest number of n digits) $= (-1)*B^n + 2*(B^n-1)/(B-1)$ $= 2*(B^n-1)/(B-1) - B^n$ We will call this number W
The difference between L and K = $= 1NN..N_N - 22..2_N$ $= B^n - 2*(B^n-1)/(B-1) - 2*(B^n-1)/(B-1)$ $= B^n - 4*(B^n-1)/(B-1)$	The difference between W and V = $= M22..2_N - NN..N_N$ $= 2*(B^n-1)/(B-1) - B^n - (-2)*(B^n-1)/(B-1)$ $= 4*(B^n-1)/(B-1) - B^n$
Equalize the difference with 1, for a valid	Equalize the difference with -1, for a valid

system. $1 = B^n - 4*(B^n-1)/(B-1)$ $4*(B^n-1)/(B-1) = B^n -1$ ∵ B cannot be 1 $4*(B^n-1) = (B^n -1)(B-1)$	system. $-1 = 4*(B^n-1)/(B-1) - B^n$ $B^n-1 = 4*(B^n-1)/(B-1)$ ∵ B cannot be 1 $(B-1)(B^n-1) = 4*(B^n-1)$
∴ $B^n - 1 = 0$ OR $4 = B-1$	
$B^n - 1 = 0$ $B^n = 1$ $n = 0$ That's rejected (meaningless)!	$4 = B-1$ **B = 5**

So, the base in the N-System is 5.

That is, for 1 digit in the N-System, we have 5 numbers: from -2 to +2.

For 2 digits in the N-System, we have 25 numbers: from -12 to +12.

To see how it works, check out the following conversion table. Visualizing a rotating odometer helps a lot here:

N system	Conversion	Decimal system
NN$_N$	-2*5-2	-12
NM$_N$	-2*5-1	-11
N0$_N$	-2*5+0	-10
N1$_N$	-2*5+1	-9
N2$_N$	-2*5+2	-8
MN$_N$	-1*5-2	-7
MM$_N$	-1*5-1	-6
M0$_N$	-1*5+0	-5
M1$_N$	-1*5+1	-4
M2$_N$	-1*5+2	-3
0N$_N$	0*5-2	-2
0M$_N$	0*5-1	-1
00$_N$	0*5+0	0

01_N	0*5+1	1
02_N	0*5+2	2
$1N_N$	1*5-2	3
$1M_N$	1*5-1	4
10_N	1*5+0	5
11_N	1*5+1	6
22_N	2*5+2	7
$2N_N$	2*5-2	8
$2M_N$	2*5-1	9
20_N	2*5+0	10
21_N	2*5+1	11
22_N	2*5+2	12

Completing the Generalization

Now, let's go one step further and try to generalize it for all possible bases.

Assuming X is a positive integer and Y = -X, the Y system will represent numbers from -X to +X using one digit.

We will use our latest equations again:

For n digits, the largest (most positive) number is $XX...X_Y$= = $X*B^0 + X*B^1 + X*B^2 + ...+ X*B^{(n-1)}$ $= X*\sum_{i=0}^{n} B^i = X*(B^n-1)/(B-1)$ We will call this number K	For n digits, the smallest (most negative) number is $YY...Y_Y$= = $(-X)*B^0 + (-X)*B^1 + (-X)*B^2 + ...+ (-X)*B^{(n-1)}$ $= \sum_{i=0}^{n}(-X)*B^i = (-X)*(B^n-1)/(B-1)$ We will call this number V
For n+1 digits, the smallest positive number is $1YY...Y_Y$ = $1*B^n$ + (the smallest number of n digits) = $1*B^n - X*(B^n-1)/(B-1)$ = $B^n - X*(B^n-1)/(B-1)$ We will call this number L	For n+1 digits, the largest negative number is $MXX...X_Y$= = $(-1)*B^n$ +(the largest number of n digits) = $(-1)*B^n + X*(B^n-1)/(B-1)$ = $X*(B^n-1)/(B-1) - B^n$ We will call this number W

The difference between L and K = $= 1YY..Y_Y - XX..X_Y$ $= B^n - X*(B^n-1)/(B-1) - X*(B^n-1)/(B-1)$ $= B^n - 4*(B^n-1)/(B-1)$	The difference between W and V = $= MXX..X_Y - YY..Y_Y$ $= X*(B^n-1)/(B-1) - B^n - (-X)*(B^n-1)/(B-1)$ $= 2X*(B^n-1)/(B-1) - B^n$
Equalize the difference with 1, for a valid system. $1 = B^n - 2X*(B^n-1)/(B-1)$ $2X*(B^n-1)/(B-1) = B^n - 1$ $\because$ B cannot be 1 $2X*(B^n-1) = (B^n - 1)(B-1)$	Equalize the difference with -1, for a valid system. $-1 = 2X*(B^n-1)/(B-1) - B^n$ $B^n-1 = 2X*(B^n-1)/(B-1)$ $\because$ B cannot be 1 $(B-1)(B^n-1) = 2X*(B^n-1)$
$\therefore B^n - 1 = 0$ OR $2X = B-1$	
$B^n - 1 = 0$ $B^n = 1$ $n = 0$ That's rejected (meaningless)!	$2X = B-1$ $\mathbf{B = 2X+1}$

Conclusion

If one digit is representing the numbers from -X to X, the base in that system is 2X+1. That is, the possible bases for positive/negative systems can only be odd numbers.

Chapter 1.07:
Expanding the Physical Examples

Expanding the Physical Examples

We have discussed two physical examples that can be used to illustrate how the BT system works: the balance scale and the odometer.

It should be easy to imagine an odometer, where each digit has 5 values, to illustrate how the N-System works.

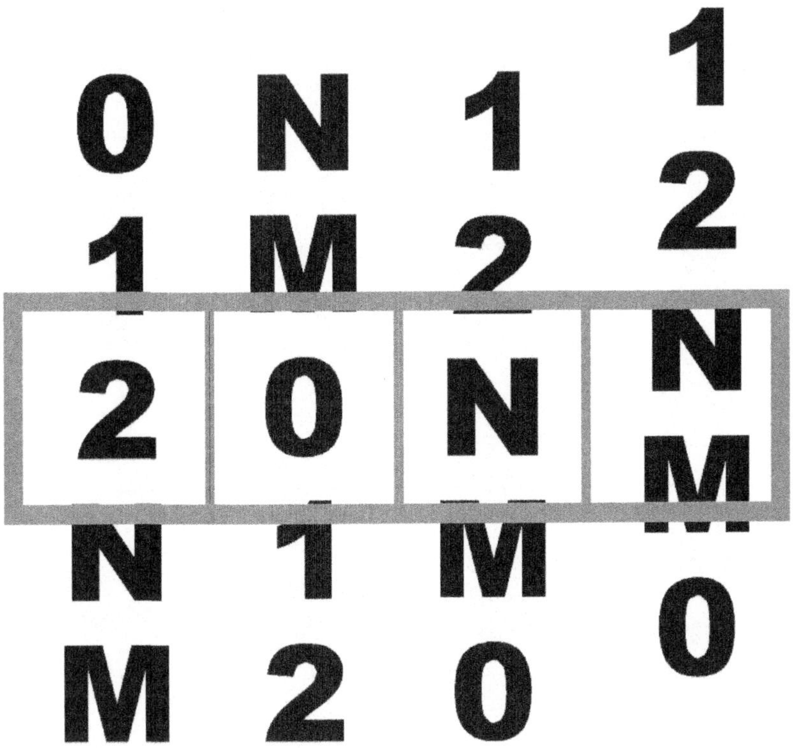

Figure 1.07.01: Hypothetical Rotating Odometer for the N-System

With the balance scale, it is a bit tricky. We mentioned that the base 3 comes from the fact that the weights can be placed in one of 3 places: the side of the fruit bag, the opposite side, and neither.

How can we find 5 possible places for the N-System in a balance scale with two sides?

Revisiting the Balance Scale

Well, to achieve balance in the scale, the rule is that the sum of each weight multiplied by its distance from the fulcrum should be equal on each side.

For example: w1*d1+w2*d2 = w3*d3+w4*d4

We can use this as follows:

There are two ways to map the BT system to the balance scale:

1) Have two pans at equal distances from the fulcrum and each weight be a multiple of 3, i.e. 1, 3, 9, 27, etc.

2) Have each weight be exactly 1 kilogram and the ability to hang it at different distances from the fulcrum. These distances should be 1, 3, 9, 27, etc.

   The bag of fruits should be hung on one side at a distance equal to 1 unit from the fulcrum. Any weight put on the same side corresponds to negative values, or Ms. Any weight put on the other side corresponds to 1. The hanging points at different distances represent the digits in the whole number.

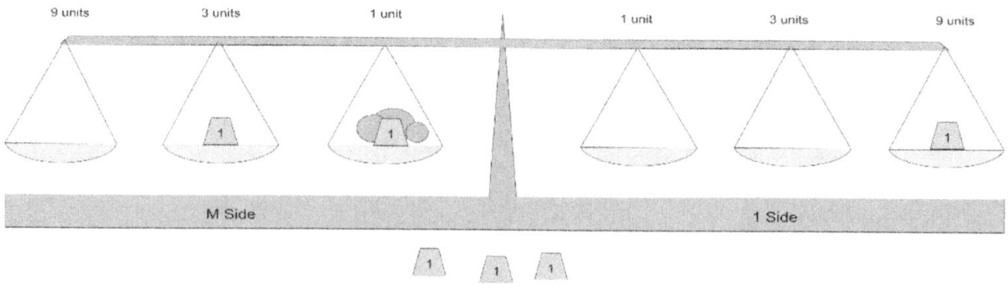

Figure 1.07.02: Balance Scale with Different Hanging Points

Example:

Use both methods (varying weights and varying distances) to achieve balance with a bag of fruits that weighs 8 kg.

[Hint: Start by converting the weight to the BT System.]

Solution #1 (varying weights):

$8 = 9 - 1 = 1*3^2 + 0*3^1 - 1*3^0 = 10M_M$

One kg will be put on the pan that has the bag of fruits and 9 kg will be put on the opposite side. The first weight represents the M, and the second weight represents the 1 in the number $10M_M$.

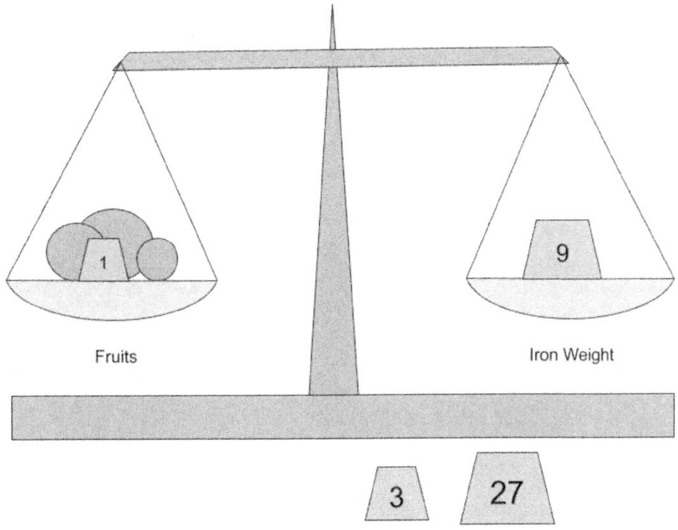

Figure 1.07.03: Balance Scale with Varying Weights, illustrating 10M.

Solution #2 (varying distances):

$8 = 9 - 1 = 1*3\^2 +0*3\^1 -1*3\^0 = 10M_M$

One kg will be hanging on the same side of the bag of fruits and at the same hanging point, i.e. 1 unit from the fulcrum, and 1 kg will be hanging on the opposite side at 9 units from the fulcrum. The first weight represents the M, and the second weight represents the 1 in the number $10M_M$.

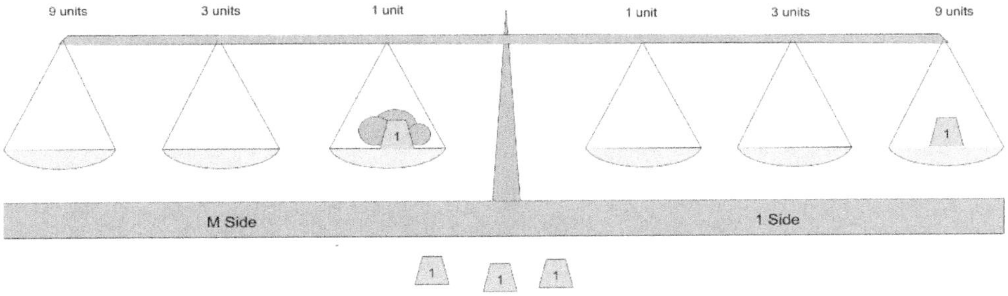

Figure 1.07.04: Balance Scale with Varying Distances, illustrating 10M.

Applying the New Method to the N-System

Now, for the N-System, we need:

1) hanging points at 1, 5, 25, and 125 units from the fulcrum on both sides.

2) weights of 1 kg and 2 kg.

- Whenever the 1 kg and 2 kg are hung on the fruit bag side they are representing M and N, respectively.
- Whenever they are hung on the opposite side, they are representing 1 and 2.
- The hanging points at different distances represent the digits in the whole number.

Example:

Using a balance scale with hanging points at 1,5, and 25 units from the fulcrum on both sides and several weights (1 kg and 2 kg) show how to achieve balance with a bag of fruits that weighs 18 kg.

[Hint: Start by converting the weight to the N-System.]

Solution:

$18 = 25-5-2 = 1*5^2 -1*5^1 -2*5^0 = 1MN_N$

- The bag of fruits should be hung at 1 unit from the fulcrum.
- At the same hanging point 2 kg should be hung, representing N in the least significant digit.
- Another 1 kg should be hung at 5 units on the same side, representing the M in the middle digit.
- 1 kg should be hung at 25 units from the fulcrum on the opposite side of the bag of the fruits.

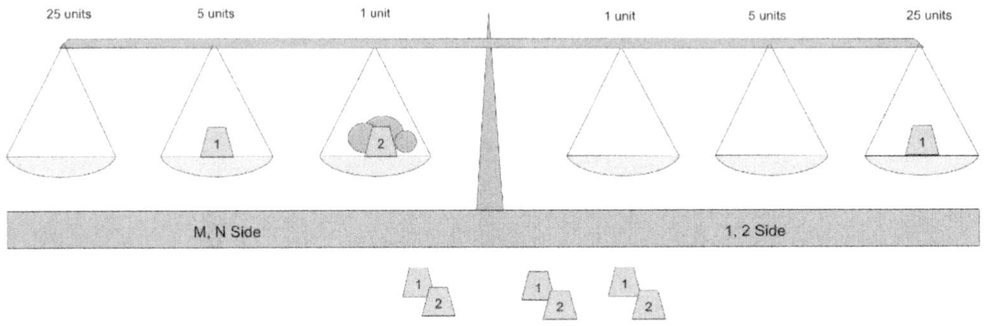

Figure 1.07.05: Balance Scale with Varying Distances, illustrating 1MN.

Four Pans

Actually, the first method of varying weights can also be expanded to illustrate the N-System. For that we need 4 pans hung as follows: two pans on each side, that's four pans: two at the same distance from the fulcrum and the other two at double of that distance. In addition, we need weights of 1 kg, 5 kg, 25 kg, 125 kg, etc.

The used pan will determine if it is N, M, 1, or 2 and the weight will determine which digit. If a weight is not used that means its corresponding digit is zero.

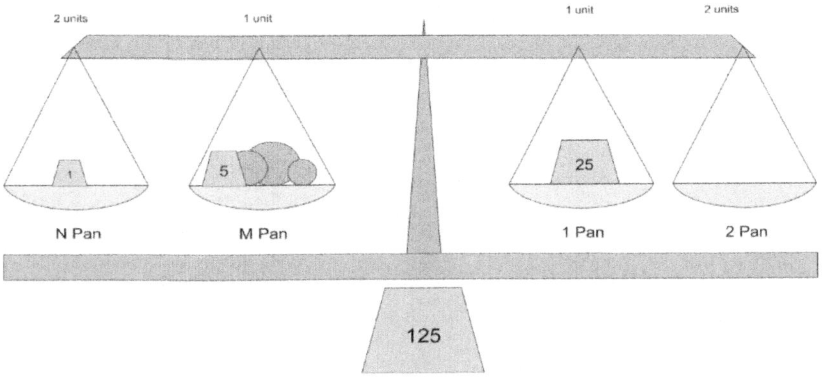

Figure 1.07.06: Balance Scale with 4 Pans

Example:

Using the above described 4 pan balance scale and weights of 1 kg, 5 kg, and 25 kg show how to achieve balance with a bag of fruits that weighs 18 kg and how this is illustrating the equivalent number in N-System.

Solution:

18 = 25-5-2 = 1*5^2 -1*5^1 -2*5^0 = $1MN_N$

- The bag of fruits should be put in the M pan, as well as the 5 kg.
- The 1 kg should be put in the N pan.
- The 25 kg should be put on the other side in the 1 pan.

1*25 +(-1)*5+(-2)*1 = 25-5-2 = 18

Voila! Balance is achieved!

Chapter 1.08:
Final Words on Part 1

Final Words on Part 1

As we have seen, throughout this part of the journey, there are similarities and differences between the balanced ternary system and the binary or ternary system. Yet all of basic math operations can be carried out.

Depending on the implementation, the balanced ternary system may prove more efficient than the binary system. Negation, for example, is more straightforward than the two's complement method.

The generalization and expansion of positive/negative systems showed that other systems are also valid.

The physical example of a four-pan balance was a good illustration that these mathematical systems have parallels in the physical world.

In part 2, we will discuss 3-value logic. We started by borrowing from Boolean logic and what they mean in the physical world, then made a shift that allowed us to make the 3-value logic more flexible and usable.

'Hope you've enjoyed this part and found it inspiring.

Printed in Great Britain
by Amazon

77183353R00032